Michael Leunig was born in Melbourne and now lives in a small rural community in north-eastern Victoria. *Curly Verse* comprises pieces that previously appeared in *The Age*, the *Sydney Morning Herald*, *Nation Review*, and various stage productions.

Also By Michael Leunig

The Penguin Leunig
The Second Leunig
The Bedtime Leunig
A Bag of Roosters
Ramming the Shears
The Travelling Leunig
A Common Prayer
The Prayer Tree
Common Prayer Collection
Introspective
A Common Philosophy
Everyday Devils and Angels
A Bunch of Poesy
You and Me
Short Notes from the Long History of Happiness
Why Dogs Sniff Each Other's Tails
Goatperson
The Curly Pyjama Letters
The Stick
Strange Creature
Wild Figments
A New Penguin Leunig
Hot
The Lot

CURLY VERSE: SELECTED POEMS

MICHAEL LEUNIG

PENGUIN BOOKS

PENGUIN BOOKS

Published by the Penguin Group
Penguin Group (Australia)
707 Collins Street, Melbourne, Victoria 3008, Australia
(a division of Penguin Australia Pty Ltd)
Penguin Group (USA) Inc.
375 Hudson Street, New York, New York 10014, USA
Penguin Group (Canada)
90 Eglinton Avenue East, Suite 700, Toronto, Canada ON M4P 2Y3
(a division of Penguin Canada Books Inc.)
Penguin Books Ltd
80 Strand, London WC2R 0RL England
Penguin Ireland
25 St Stephen's Green, Dublin 2, Ireland
(a division of Penguin Books Ltd)
Penguin Books India Pvt Ltd
11 Community Centre, Panchsheel Park, New Delhi – 110 017, India
Penguin Group (NZ)
67 Apollo Drive, Rosedale, Auckland 0632, New Zealand
(a division of Penguin New Zealand Pty Ltd)
Penguin Books (South Africa) (Pty) Ltd,
Rosebank Office Park, Block D, 181 Jan Smuts Avenue, Parktown North,
Johannesburg, 2196, South Africa
Penguin (Beijing) Ltd
7F, Tower B, Jiaming Center, 27 East Third Ring Road North,
Chaoyang District, Beijing 100020, China

Penguin Books Ltd, Registered Offices: 80 Strand, London, WC2R 0RL, England

First published as *Poems: 1972–2002* by Penguin Group (Australia), 2003
This revised edition published by Penguin Group (Australia), 2010

Text copyright © Michael Leunig 2003

The moral right of the author has been asserted

Typeset in 13.5/20 pt Perpetua by Post Pre-Press Group, Brisbane, Australia
Printed and bound in Australia by Griffin Press

National Library of Australia
Cataloguing-in-Publication data:

Leunig, Michael, 1945–
Curly verse: selected poems/Michael Leunig.
2nd ed.
9780143204756 (pbk.)
Previously published: Poems 1972–2002. Viking, 2003.

A821.3

penguin.com.au

Sitting on the Fence

Come sit down beside me,
I said to myself,
And although it doesn't make sense,
I held my own hand
As a small sign of trust
And together I sat on the fence.

Duck Study

How you will know
If a person,
Perhaps a politician, a policeman,
A partner or a priest,
Is corrupt:

You must study the duck.
You must play with the duck.
You must talk with the duck.
You must know the ways of the duck.
You must look deeply into the eyes of the
    duck.
Then, looking into the face of the person,
How will you know if that person is corrupt?
You will know.
YOU WILL KNOW.

True Happiness

How may a man measure his own happiness?
He must first go to his cupboard
and take out all his neckties.
Then he must lay them out on the ground
End to end.
Then he must measure the length of this line
  of neckties,
And that measurement,
That distance,
Is exactly the same as his distance from true
  happiness.

A Book

On the armchair, a book:
How to Relax.
Beside the bed, a book:
How to Get to Sleep.
Next to the window, a book:
How to See What's in Front of You.
Next to the man, a book:
How to be a Man.
On the desk, a book:
How to Succeed in Life.
In hell, a book:
How You Ended up in Hell.

No Sooner

No sooner do you arrive than it's time to
   leave.
How beautiful it is, how glorious,
Yet it's nearly time to go.
So you take it in, you take it in.

And you take a few small souvenirs,
Some leaves: lavender, rosemary, eucalyptus;
A few small pebbles, a few small secrets,
A look you received, nine little notes of music,
And then it's time to go.

You move towards the open door
And the silent night beyond,
The few bright stars, a deep breath,
And it really is time to go.

No sooner does it all begin to make sense
Does it start to come true,
Does it all open up,
Do you begin to see,
Does it enter into your heart . . .
No sooner do you arrive than it's time to
    leave.

Yes, it's the truth.
And then you will have passed through it,
And with mysterious consequence
It will have passed through you.

A Dusty Little Swag

All my father left me
Was a dusty little swag
And a pair of tiny booties
In a crumpled paper bag,
And he left me in confusion
And he left me in despair
And he left the swag and booties
For the walk to God knows where.

Let It Go

Let it go,
Let it out,
Let it all unravel;
Let it free
And it will be
A path on which to travel.

At the Top

At the top of the tallest building in the world
Sat the saddest man in the world
And inside the man
Was the loneliest heart in the world
And inside the heart
Was the deepest pit in the world
And at the bottom of the pit
Was the blackest mud in the world
And in the mud lay the lightest,
loveliest, tenderest,
Most beautiful, happy angel in the universe.

Autumn

Leaves are falling and revealing
One of winter's eerie sights:
On the trees, how unappealing,
Wire for the fairy lights.

Wire with plastic insulation
Stapled onto every limb;
Circuits in the vegetation
Indicate that life is grim.

Misery in any city
Can be measured, if you please,
By counting with the eye of pity
Fairy lights installed in trees.

Magpie

Magpie, magpie, dive on me,
Swoop down from your holy tree;
As I pass the flower bed
Stick your beak into my head.

Magpie, magpie, make a hole,
Through my head into my soul;
As I pass beneath the sun
Bring my troubled head undone.

Magpie, magpie, it is spring,
Is my soul a happy thing?
As I pass around the tree
Make a hole so you can see.

Hair

We give thanks for the mystery of hair:
Too little here and too much there,
Censored and shaved, controlled and
   suppressed,
Unwelcome guest in soups and sandwiches,
Difficult growth always needing attention,
Gentle and comforting, complex and wild,
Reminding us softly that we might be animals,
Growing and growing 'til the day that we die
And the day after as well, so they say.

In all of its places, in all of its ways,
We give thanks for the blessing of hair.

Common Sense

Cross my heart, I remember
When common sense was delivered to the door
Each morning by horse and cart,
Equally to the rich and poor.

What a bold start it was
To find it sitting there on the porch,
All yours, fresh as a daisy
And as good as gold.

Completely undebated was common sense;
Unprocessed, you might say,
Full of organisms and rough seeds.
It's what the body needs.
You could feel it do you good.

How could
Such a useful thing,

So plentiful back then
Yet so revered,
Become so lost and rare
And so weird?

You have to go through so much these days,
Crawl across a field of broken bottles,
Half a life of suffering and sin,
Be done over and done in
Before you find it once again.

Perhaps one morning
On the porch
And in the sun of early spring,
Lo and behold,
On the step, thank Christ,
A little common sense is there again.

A Winter's Poem

A clever creature is the snake,
Who spends his winter not awake;
He snuggles in his long thin bed
And brews up venom in this head.

The human is a different sort;
He spends the winter watching sport;
He yells abuse in concrete stands
And empties out his poison glands.

Upon the Sagging Mattress

Upon the sagging mattress known as life
The weary husband lays down with his wife
To feel the nasty shapes and awful lumps
To get no rest, to only get the grumps.

And yet upon this drooping bag of woe
They close their eyes and sometimes have a go
At fantasising sweeter, better things:
A life with good support and inner springs.

A Little Duck

With a bit of luck
A duck
Will come into your life.

When you are at the peak
Of your great powers,
And your achievement towers
Like a smoking chimney stack,
There'll be a quack
And right there at your feet
A little duck will stand;
She will take you by the hand
And lead you

Like a child with no defence;
She will lead you
Into wisdom, joy and innocence.
That little duck.

I wish you luck.

The Inner Horse

You can lead a horse to water
But you can't make it cheerful;
The bucket is full
But the horse is tearful,
So you give it a loving earful:
'What's up, old fellah?' you say.
He looks at you and looks away.
Of course.
The dear old inner horse.

He Was a Man

In Menswear
He shot a brightly coloured sportscoat
With his trusty bow.

He harpooned
A large, fat couch
In the furniture department.

He clubbed
A pop-up toaster
In the electrical section.

With his bare hands
He fought a king-size quilt
In Bedding.

He cast his net in Footwear

And caught

A magnificent pair of slippers.

He was a hunter.

He was a provider.

He was a MAN.

Here I Am (manifesto)

Here I am,
Alive on earth.
Conscious,
Unconscious,
Semi-conscious.
Knowing others,
Known to others,
Yet also unknowable
And alone forever.
Soon I will not be here.
Hurrah!

How to Get There

Go to the end of the path until you get to the
   gate.

Go through the gate and head straight out
   towards the horizon.

Keep going towards the horizon.

Sit down and have a rest every now and again,
But keep on going, just keep on with it.

Keep on going as far as you can.

That's how you get there.

How to Hold Onto It

Hold onto it like you hold a day-old chicken.

Hold onto it like you hold a live fish.

Hold onto it like you hold a horse.

Hold onto it like you hold a bowl of soup.

Hold onto it like you hold a door open for the
   Queen Mother.

Letting go of it is just as difficult

And shall be dealt with at some later stage.

Ceremony

We are gathered here
To witness the marriage
Of Fiona and Simon.

Simon, do you accept
That you are a complete jerk?
'I do.'

And do you, Fiona, accept
That you are an absolute bitch?
'I do.'

I now declare you married
In the full sense.
Congratulations.

A Biography

He took it like a man
Right on the chin,
And when he was older
His jaw caved in.

She took it politely
With a sweet smile,
But when she was older
She was thoroughly vile.

They took their revenge
And got very rich,
The chinless wonder
And the vile old bitch.

Homes Are Quietly Burning

Homes are quietly burning,
Madness on the march,
Lies move unresisted through the land.
We stand helpless as our lives are occupied
Faster than we understand.
Collaborators wave their little flags
As ugliness takes over.
'Make a friend of ugliness,' they say.
'Learn the language, then you won't get hurt.'

But you will,
No matter how you crawl.
A knock on the door one night,
A scuffle in the hall,
Your heart rubbed in the dirt.
'All right!' you scream your indecision,
'Take the children but leave the television.'

So you stand by useless
As childhood is trashed,
Innocence reviled,
The truth is bashed.
The home and the idea of home
Is set on fire, and still you stand by
As the goodness in your culture burns.
You stand there in the glow,
Going, going,
Going with the flow.

Ah yes, the flow. Heaven help us!

One day you might be asked,
'How come you didn't know what was going
  on?
Why did you not fight?'

'Fight?' you'll say. 'That's a word that never
  occurred.'

The very word brings tears.
It will dawn on you after all those painful
  years
That to fight is one of the most beautiful,
  simple, and useful ideas.

Literature

The pen is mightier than the sword
And mightier than the literary award;
Without the pen we'd be unable
To leave those notes on the kitchen table:
Nothing lovelier ever penned,
With three small crosses at the end,
Made for no one else to see,
The literature of you and me.

Little Tendrils

Little tendrils of the heart
Curling out and groping,
Seeking little things to hold,
Wiggling and hoping.

Little tendrils of the soul
Delicate and perky,
Seeking little surfaces
Peculiar and quirky.

Little tendrils, little tendrils,
Innocent and plucky, I pray that you are
   careful
And I hope that you are lucky.

Scraps

Little scraps of peace and quiet,
Hope, conversation, handshakes —
All in dribs and drabs.
A few crumbs of fun,
A tiny flake of beauty,
One teaspoon of enthusiasm —
Offcuts of each other.
A skerrick of community,
A bit of a kiss.
A snippet of eye contact,
A snippet of hospitality,
A snippet of patience,
A shred of honour,
A wisp of good humour,
A sample of compassion —
Leftovers, oddments,

Remnants of the glorious situation.
A fragment of God,
Not much, really.
Sorry, time's up.

Love is Born

Love is born
With a dark and troubled face,
When hope is dead
And in the most unlikely place;
Love is born,
Love is always born.

The Bottle

I met a man perched on a bottle
With a woman deep inside,
Rising slowly up towards him,
Floating on the tears he cried.

Said he, 'It's only tears can save her,
Tears of sorrow, tears of pain.
I'm going to have to feel a lot,
Until I have her back again.'

All sniffling and snuffling,
He said, 'It almost makes me laugh
To think that if you weep enough
A man can find his better half.'

Us

Last night while looking at the sky
I saw a little planet die.
It died and fell without a fuss;
I wondered whether it was us,
Or part of us that I had seen
Disintegrate. It could have been.

Mother Earth

Poor old lonely mother earth
Is very, very sad;
She had a bomb put in her heart
By people who are mad.
She held them and she fed them,
She taught them to be free;
They put a bomb inside her heart
And whispered, *'C'est la vie.'*

Modern Stupid

It's much easier
To be stupid these days
Than in previous times.

Back in the old days
They had to do it all by hand.
It was sheer drudgery.

Now we can do it faster
And with more comfort,
Thanks to modern methods.

You can fit it into a busy life,
It's available to everyone.
It's right there at your fingertips.

My Big Toe

My big toe is an honest man,
So down to earth and normal,
Always true unto himself
And pleasantly informal.
Full of simple energy,
Contented with his role.
If all of me could be like him
I'd be a happy soul.

Ode to Her Majesty

I did but see her passing by, she passed me by
  quite fast.
I saw her passing by again when several years
  had passed.
And then at some much later stage she passed
  me by once more
And there were further passings-by and these
  I also saw.
I did but see her passing by, I don't know what
  it means;
Perhaps it's not my problem, but a problem of
  the Queen's.

Mr Rabbit

Mr Rabbit came to Australia with his wife
To raise a family and make a brand new life.
'Let us rejoice for we are young and free,'
He said while touching Mrs Rabbit on the
   knee.
They rushed ashore and quickly dug a hole,
Then lay down side by side and lost control.

My Shoe

Since I hurt my pendulum
My life is all erratic,
My parrot who was cordial
Is now transmitting static.
The carpet died, a palm collapsed,
The cat keeps doing poo;
The only thing that keeps me sane
Is talking to my shoe.

Our Father

A spectacular event
Which suddenly surpasses
The great news stories of the world:

Our father,
Normally a worried and serious man,
Does an underwater handstand
In the bay.

Peace

Peace is my drug;
It stops the pain.
In safe reflecting rooms
Or in a lane,
Or in a park,
I will lie
And have some peace
And get high.

If it's pure
And there's a lot of it about
I overdose
And pass out
And dream of peace:
My favourite thing
When nobody wants me
And nothing's happening.

Artist, Leave the World of Art

Artist, leave the world of art,
Pack your goodies on a cart,
Duck out through some tiny hole,
Slip away and save your soul.

Leave no footprints, don't look back,
Take the dark and dirty track.
Cross the border, cross your heart:
Freedom from the world of art.

Anthem

Underpants which have in winter sagged
And fallen into darkness and despond
Shall from their shame and loneliness be
   dragged
And laid upon the fern's emerging frond.
The frond shall gently rise to greet the spring,
Above the flowers into the sun fantastic,
Where birds in praise of underpants shall sing
And life shall be restored to old elastic.
Yes, life shall be restored to old elastic.

Tiny Boat

God bless this tiny little boat
And me who travels in it;
It stays afloat for years and years
And sinks within a minute.

And so the soul in which we sail
Unknown by years of thinking
Is deeply felt and understood
The minute that it's sinking.

Moments of no Consequence

Moments of no consequence
Seem to make a lot of sense,
Like the gentle pitter-patter
Of the things that do not matter,
As I sit alone and stare,
Neither here and neither there.

Such a Fuss

Each day — such a fuss,
Such praise, such damnation:
Ooh, ahh, yes, no . . . !
Exhaustion and disintegration.

Such a fuss, yet the goat
Eats little flowers and thorns
And hears the sparrow
Singing brightly in his horns
(The sun is sweet, the afternoon lies sleeping
  in the valley),
A song for little flowers and thorns
Digesting in the belly.

The Awfulisers

Every night and every day
The awfulisers work away,
Awfulising public places,
Favourite things and little graces;
Awfulising lovely treasures,
Common joys and simple pleasures;
Awfulising far and near
The parts of life we held so dear:
Democratic, clean and lawful,
Awful, awful, awful, awful.

The Empty Jeff

An empty Jeff came through the clouds
And hung there for a minute,
A vacuum in the shape of Jeff
With no Jeff in it!

'The empty Jeff, the empty Jeff,'
The people cried in awe,
All staring at the space where Jeff
Was very much no more.

Ode to a Jet-ski Person

Jet-ski person, selfish fink,
May your silly jet-ski sink,
May you hit a pile of rocks,
Oh hoonish, summer, coastal pox.

Noisy, smoking, dickhead fool
On your loathsome leisure tool,
Give us all a jolly lark
And sink beside a hungry shark.

Scream as in its fangs you go,
Your last attention-seeking show,
While on the beach we all join in
With 'Three cheers for the dorsal fin!'

Robin Hood

Robin Hood, Robin Hood,
You'd be napalmed in the wood,
I am very sad to say,
If you were alive today.

Gratitude and Grief

In the cradle of his mother's arms a baby lies
Warm and sheltered from the time when they
    will come apart
Gazing from the hidden world into his
    mother's eyes
From where the holy secrets tumble down
    into his heart.

Then with this heart so full of hope he travels
    in the wild
But soon is set upon and cruelly beaten to the
    ground
And wakes upon the ruins of his innocence
    defiled
And there his sacred revelations in the mud
    are found.

Tears of blood and anger flowing from his
   wounded eye
From his violated mouth the song of disbelief
In his shattered memory a shattered lullaby
But from his broken heart flow gratitude and
   grief.

Woes Maketh the Man

Woes maketh the man.
A troubled heart on a well-cut sleeve,
A well-cut lip, a loose weave,
A sock on the jaw,
A pullover,
A fallover on the floor,
A collar well pressed
Against the wall,
Another cuff, another fall,
A good belt, a black tie,
A black eye, a huge welt,
A felt hat, a hate deeply felt,
A fate with a rip in the rear,
A nicely stitched ear,
A scarf to match the scar,
A scarlet scratch upon the cheek,

A splash of crimson from the nose.

Ah yes,

What maketh the man is his woes.

The Golden Thread

I'm looking for life's precious little golden
thread.

*We've got the rusty chain, the tangled wire, the
thick rope,*

*But we can't help you with the golden thread, I'm
afraid.*

What do you want it for?

I want to just see it, I want to smile at it.

I want to tell life's precious little golden
thread that I love it.

That's all I want.

*We've got the ball of string, the reel of packaging
tape and the optic fibre cable,*

But I'm sorry,

We don't have the golden thread any more.

The Home for the Appalled

They took him on a stretcher
To the Home for the Appalled
Where he lay down in a corner
And he bawled and bawled and bawled.

'There's nothing wrong with me,' he wailed,
When asked about his bawling,
'It's the world that needs attention;
It's so utterly appalling.'

'It's so utterly appalling,'
He sobbed and cried and bawled,
And the chorus rose to join him
At the Home for the Appalled.

The Crowdless Man

See him wandering alone,
The crowdless man,
He has no group,
He has no tribe,
He carries his identity in his pocket.
His pocket has a hole in it,
His story has a hole in it,
His tragedy is not a tune you can hum.
His suffering and sacrifice,
They have no handles;
His persecution has no logo,
No shrine, no yardstick.
His joy has no credentials,
His observations have no fixed address;
There are no awards whatsoever.

His gaze and yearning are way outside the
  loop,
His pilgrimage has lots of holes in it.
See him wandering alone
Beaming to himself.

The Gentle Hum

I wonder,
Will it all click into place?
I feel it might.
I had a glimpse
That things could all come right.
I'd wake up
On a sunny, slightly roostered morn
And wouldn't realise at first;
The rightness would take time to dawn.
And gradually
The thing would start to gleam;
This worried life I'd had,
This awful world, this painful mess —
It was, in fact, a kind of dream.
The penny would just drop
Into my hand,
The penny that I'd lost so long ago,

And all the peace withheld and blocked from
  me
Would start to flow.
The gentle hum, the gold and silver light
Would all resume;
The fairies and the pixies,
The particles of dust
Caught in the sunlight in my room.
I'd pick up
Where I'd been so rudely interrupted;
I'd have it back again for keeps,
My dog, my brilliant grasp of life,
My backyard and my paddocks full of time,
The world all glad around me,
My rightful place,
My joyous leaps.

A Child is a Grub

A child is a grub,
A man's a cocoon,
Music's a butterfly . . .
Sing me a tune.

Christmas

I see a twinkle in your eye,
So this shall be my Christmas star
And I will travel to your heart:
The manger where the real things are.

And I will find a mother there
Who holds you gently to her breast,
A father to protect your peace,
And by these things you shall be blessed.

And you will always be reborn
And I will always see the star
And make the journey to your heart:
The manger where the real things are.

The Plot

'He's lost the plot,' they say,
But it simply isn't true;
You cannot lose the plot,
It's stuck to you!

Nor can it be chucked out
Or thrown into a pit;
You can't just dump the plot,
You're stuck to it!

But you can soak the plot
And loosen it with tears
And slowly peel it back.
It could take years.

And you can lose your face
And you can lose a lot
And feel blessed when they say,
'He's lost the plot!'

Doom and Gloom

On the bus
The smell of doom hung heavily in the air.
At the office, the smell of doom!
In the coffee shop, everywhere he went,
The unmistakable smell of doom.

Even at home, at the dinner table,
The all-pervasive, inescapable smell of doom.
And in his bedroom too,
The appalling, repulsive smell
Of doom and gloom.

Then he noticed
It was stuck to the bottom of his shoe.
He had trodden in it!

The Other You

And who is that happy soul beside you,
So unabashed,
Holding that great big bunch of flowers,
Holding your arm,
Singing that trashy song you secretly love,
The trashy song that brings you to a halt,
Brings you to your knees,
Brings you to your precious tears of happiness?
Who is that?

Who is that tickling the palm of your hand
And whispering in your ear,
'Yes, go on, I dare you'?
Who is it that clears your mess while you
    sleep,
Who waits calmly for your awakening,
Who loves you from afar?

Could it be . . . ?

Could it possibly be . . . ?

Yes, it is.

Of course it is.

It's the other you!

The Horse I Backed

The only horse I ever backed
Turned and ran the other way.
At the very start it turned and jumped a fence
And was gone from sight.

A week later I saw it
High in the mountains,
Still going strong.
It leapt a huge chasm
And disappeared from sight.

About a year later I saw it
Struggling through heavy seas,
Far from land but looking good,
Looking good.

Years passed
And then I saw it
Galloping through a terrible fire.
I saw it chased by mad dogs.

And then . . .
I saw it in a green pasture;
It was looking good, looking good.

The horse I backed
Took a different course.

The Value of the Soul

The value of the soul plunged yesterday
To its lowest level in five years.
One person invested in a smile.
A meteor plummeted and a few wishes were
   made.
Experts said nothing.
There were rumours about a small child
Who had flown over the city on a carpet of
   rose petals.
Certain things slid and crashed,
But a cheer rose up and a dog barked.
A violin was heard too.

The Kitchen of Give and Take

First you must climb into the battered old
  saucepan of love
Where you will marinate in the sauce of sex.
Then you shall be covered with the wine of
  faith,
The oil of compassion
And the salt of suffering and sin.

Now you are tossed in the pan of chaos
And seared by the flame of truth.
You are carved by the knife of compromise
And served with the spoon of duty
Onto the plate of acceptance
And garnished with the herbs of humility.
At this point you may well say grace.

The Path to Your Door

The path to your door
Is the path within,
Is made by animals,
Is lined by thorns,
Is stained with wine,
Is lit by the lamp of sorrowful dreams,
Is washed with joy,
Is swept by grief,
Is blessed by the lonely traffic of art,
Is known by heart,
Is known by prayer,
Is lost and found,
Is always strange,
The path to your door.

The Missile

There is a missile, so I've heard,
Which locks on to the smallest bird,
Finely tuned to seek and kill
A tiny chirp or gentle trill.

It's modern warfare's answer to
An ancient wisdom tried and true:
When fighting wars you first destroy
All songs of innocence and joy.

Life is Offensive and Refuses to Apologise

The rose bush:
An arch-conservative with cruel thorns.
Death:
The right-wing radical.

The heartless, dull bureaucracy of time.

The cat?
The cat is probably a monarchist!
The dog?
A moral vacuum, an uneducated, pleasure-driven philistine.

And the moon . . .
So aloof, so cold, so full of itself.

The Poppy

The poppy pod is cut and seeps,
The tiny child is crushed and weeps.
The child is crushed and crushed again
To make a special type of pain,
The agony which cannot weep
But tries to rock itself to sleep.
The poppy's weeping does become
A special kind of opium.
Then the child will pluck the flower,
Each the other to devour;
Asleep together in the wild,
The poppy and the little child.

Real and Right and True

Go your way now,
All shall be well.
Leave the day now,
All shall be well.
Go into the darkness
Where the spark is,
Real and right and true.

Tiny baby
Taught you to cry.
Tiny birdie
Taught you to fly
Out into the brightness
Where the light is,
Real and right and true.

La-La Land

I want to go to La-La Land
And have a holiday;
In La-La Land they'll understand
The thing I have to say.

I'll rent the little wonky shack
That overlooks the bay
And wait until it all comes back,
This thing I have to say.

And then one night I'll bow my head
While strolling on the sand
And say the thing that must be said
Out loud in La-La Land.

The Summer Palace

Make a little garden in your pocket,
Fill your cuffs with radishes and rocket,
Let a passionfruit crawl up your thigh,
Grow some oregano in your fly.

Make a steamy compost of your fears,
Trickle-irrigate your life with tears,
Let your troubled mind become a trellis,
Turn your heart into a summer palace.

The Swan

The Australian swan is rather drack
Dressed in dusty charcoal black,
But it is graceful,
With its face full of serious intent;
And though its neck is curved,
Its life is bent
On living out its ancient destiny
And sailing out upon a sea
Of self-reflection
Where blackness is perfection.

Things Just Seem to Fall Apart

Things just seem to fall apart,
String bags full of oranges
And things within the heart;
Calamities evaporate and memories depart.
People laugh at anything
And things just fall apart.

The Pie of Life

The pie of life
Is hurled into your face
Every day,
But that is no disgrace.

A life worth living
Gets splattered on your shirt,
And though you're shocked
And rather deeply hurt,
These pies of life
Which fly out of the blue —
You're made for them
And they were made for you.

We Are Accepting

We loosen our grip,
We open our hand,
We are accepting.

In our empty hand
We feel the shape
Of simple eternity.

It nestles there;
We hold it gently,
We are accepting.

What Did You Get?

What did you get on your Christmas morn,
On the Christmas morn when you were born?
Did you get some milk?
Did you get some pain?
Did you get some hurt that you can't explain?
Did you get a star from high above?
Did you get the gaze of a mother's love –
The spark that leaps from eye to eye
And twinkles 'til the day you die?

Oh, what did we get on our Christmas morn,
On the Christmas morn when we were born?

The Festival of Art

Artist, artist in your garret
With your pussy cat and parrot,
Why are you not taking part
In the Festival of Art?

Here's the reason I'm not part
Of the Festival of Art:
I am feasting in my garret
With my pussy cat and parrot.

When the Heart

When the heart
Is cut or cracked or broken,
Do not clutch it;
Let the wound lie open.

Let the wind
From the good old sea blow in
To bathe the wound with salt,
And let it sting.

Let a stray dog lick it,
Let a bird lean in the hole and sing
A simple song like a tiny bell,
And let it ring.

Why Do We Do It?

Nobody seems to know
Why we do it.
Nobody seems to even ask
Why we do it.
No voice of gentle enquiry,
No bewildered cry from the street,
The sudden shout,
'Why do we do it?'

How strange!
It's as if everybody knows
Precisely why we do it,
And the reason is too obvious to mention,
Or perhaps too vile and shameful to
   acknowledge,
Or too silly.
Why the silence?

Do we do it because everybody else does it,
Or is it because we are afraid of not doing it?

Why?
Please!
Somebody!
Why do we do it?

The Warlords of Suburbia

The warlords of suburbia
Sitting on their couches
With lots of ammunition in their pouches.

'Death to the enemy!'
Is the warlord's cry; and
'I think I'll have another lovely piece of pie.'

'Take his life!' mumbles the warlord.
'He's an evil swine!
Why should he have it?
I didn't have mine.'

From the tiny balcony
That overlooks the neighbour's pool,
The warlord of suburbia dreams
Of a concrete busting bomb
And begins to drool.

'Free the Arab women from the veil!'
Speaks the warlord to his wife,
Thinking how she'd benefit
From the plastic surgeon's knife.

Then the warlord of suburbia
Totters off to bed
And lies there wondering
About being dead.

Women's Poem

All men are bastards.
We will fight for equality
Until
All women are bastards too.

Writer

Is there in this life a nook
Not described in some damned book?
Or in the heart a little bird
Not yet captured by a word?
Or in the soul a tiny breath
Which hasn't been described to death?
Something lovelier and lighter
Than the craft of some damned writer?

What's the Use?

What's the use of this little hand;
What's the use of this little eye;
What's the use of this little mouth
When all the world is broken?

Make a cake with this little hand;
Make a tear with this little eye;
Make a word with this little mouth
When all the world is broken.

Rejoice!

The people in your world (including you),
They are your humble ration in this life;
This flaky, raggle-taggle, motley crew,
Your nasty husband and your silly wife.

Your lovely wife, your darling husband too,
Your happy neighbour sobbing on all fours –
Oh, the sweet and feeble things they do.
You are theirs, alas, and they are yours.

And you are yours as well and you are you,
And all that's left of you (your dwindling
   passion).
Rejoice, rejoice whatever else you do,
Rejoice and nibble sweetly on your ration.

A Life

Anyone can get a life,
Anyone can lose it,
But who will dare to inhabit the thing
And use it?

A lived-in life
Will soon get loose and worn
From use and feeling:
Countless tiny scratches,
The shine goes off,
It's very unappealing!

Dirt builds up,
A load of muck and grit;
A part of you gets lost:
A hope, a philosophy,
Or a love that doesn't fit.

Another broken sleep,
A dream collapses;

A quick repair, it's worth a try.
A scrap of string from the soul,
Perhaps a battered grin will fill the hole.
Or just a sigh.

Flakes and cracks!
A major idea buckles badly,
A makeshift support is put up quickly;
A tired old joke could hide the dint,
Or be a wedge or a patch or a splint,
Truly, sweetly, sadly.

And yet it works and lives!
It all still goes. It forgives.
It's a miracle!
Worn in, bashed in, cried in,
And the great thing –
A lived-in life can be happily died in.

Mushrooms

Mushrooms are amazing folk,
Up into the world they poke;
Clean and tender, bold and pert,
Magic from the autumn dirt.

Mushrooms, I can feel for you,
All your work of pushing through;
Pushing through the heavy dirt,
Clean and tender, bold and pert.

Happiness

Happiness is just a little thing;
Humans mostly are too large for it.
If you cannot feel the joy of spring
Shrink yourself and maybe then you'll fit.

Autumn Poem

The pen is mightier than the gourd
But the gourd is more contented
And beautiful and self-assured;
The pen is more tormented.
It craves to make its mark and then
It dreads to be ignored;
I want to be less of a pen
And be more of a gourd.

A Gloom

A gloom of one's own,
A picture or two,
A chair by the window,
A sad little view
Of yourself passing by
In the street all alone —
What a wonderful thing
Is a gloom of one's own.

Billy the Rabbit

Billy the rabbit is dead.
He died in his cage on a cool afternoon
With Sarah the guinea pig
There by his side.

The girl who had named him
And cuddled him joyfully
Came home from school and discovered him
Lying there pitifully, beautifully:
Billy the rabbit uncuddled and dead.

'Billy,' she cried, and everything broke
As she broke down and gathered up Sarah
And walked through the rain,
Sobbing, 'Billy, poor Billy is dead.'

It's evening
And Billy is lying in state on the verandah,
All speckled with petals,
Surrounded by freshly picked grasses and
   flowers
In a fruit box with one little wobbly candle
Casting some light on a note at his feet:

   'Dear Billy, I couldn't stop crying when you died,
   I am so sorry for Sarah and you . . .'

And there was her name
And a drawing of Billy, all smiling, Signed
   with new meaning and mystery;
The name of the girl who had come home to
   find
That Billy the rabbit was dead.

The Wagon of Hope

The wagon of hope
Is pulled by ducks,
Two fine ducks
As white as snow.
The boat of faith
Is kept afloat
By stars above
And fish below.
The way ahead
Is known to birds,
Is told by birds
Each day at dawn.
The song of doom
Composed by men
Is played upon
A paper horn.

Well-Connected Goat

I saw a goat one frosty morn
With a moon upon his horn,
With a star upon his tail,
With a bird upon his back,
With a flower upon his nose,
With his feet upon a rock,
With his eyes upon the ground,
With the frost upon his coat.
Good morning, well-connected goat.

Shopping

Fools rush in where angels fear to shop.
Shopping is the best form of defence.
When the cats away the mice will shop.
Shops will be shops.
Better to have shopped and lost
Than never to have shopped at all.

Shopping is the infinite capacity to take pains.
A little shop is a dangerous thing.
He who hesitates is shopping.
Shopping men tell no tales.
There is always room at the shop.
Shopping is stranger than fiction.

Hell hath no fury like a woman shopping.
The husband is always the last to shop.
To shop is human.
Any shop in a storm.

Shop and the world shops with you,
Weep and you weep alone.

The customer is always shopping.
Shop and let shop.
Whom the gods would destroy they first send
  shopping.
You cannot run with the hares and shop with
  the hounds.
Empty shops make the most sound.
Shop and ye shall find.

Vote

Little tiny precious vote,
Underneath my overcoat,
Snug and warm against my heart,
You and I will have to part.

I must cast you to the horde,
With your little wooden sword,
And your hopeful marching song;
Little vote of mine be strong.

Should our happy cause be dashed,
And your wooden sword be smashed,
Come back, dear beloved vote,
Dream inside my overcoat.

The Smile

I shot a smile into the air
It fell to earth I know not where
Perhaps on someone else's face
In some forgotten, quiet place.

Perhaps somewhere a sleeping child
Has had a happy dream and smiled
Or some old soul about to die
Has smiled and made a little sigh.

Has sighed a simple final prayer
That lifts up gently in the air
And flows into the world so wild,
Perhaps to wake the sleeping child.

Love One Another

Love one another
And you will be happy.
It's as simple and as difficult as that.
There is no other way.

The Art World

On one hand we have the world.
Five trillion light-years away is the art world.

The art world has no gravity and no up or
   down.
It is made of gas and revolves around a black
   hole.

It was formed when a vacuum exploded
After colliding with a cosmic silence
That was expanding backwards into itself.

This caused a chaotic implosion of vaporised
   antimatter
That emitted random, light-charged time
   particles
And formed a perpetually disintegrating
   vortex.

This is how the art world was created
And this is pretty much how it remains to
 this day.

The Intriguer

Uncanny and unseen, the Intriguer visits your
   life,
Leaving peculiar shadows and odd little signs.
Clues and omens, fragments of revelation,
Strange marks and mysterious rearrangements.

Such are his works — works of genius,
Yet none of it adds up or shows the way.
A spout falls off a teapot in a quiet room,
A white pillow drops from the sky.

He moves lightly.

A ukulele goes out of tune on Sunday. Every
   Sunday!
Soon you surrender to the eerie inspiration of
   the Intriguer,

The unseen one, the brilliant disturber.
His sparkle is everywhere but he is nowhere to
   be found.

Homeland

Homeland, yes,
For better or for worse,
Homeland it is!

To know and be known by . . .
To feel for . . .
Be drawn to . . .
Be lost in . . .
Be held by . . .
To be thrown through time
And loved and decomposed in . . .
Recomposed in . . .
Dreamed and breathed in . . .
Grown and ground into the land.

The little stone —
The million years of memory
In the little stone;

Radiant the little stone . . .
We listen to the memory of the little stone,
The stone that lies upon the dust,
The dust that we become . . .
From where we come . . .
The dust and rain of homeland.

Homeland is a little stone
And love is dust
That settles on a hand,
Upon a life;
A little life that falls upon the land.

At last,
A little rain;
How radiant the little stone,
The little life ground into dust
And into layers,

Into hills
And memories and clouds —
The dust upon the hand
Is homeland.

Presidents and Prime Ministers

Presidents and Prime Ministers are
   magnificent creatures
They're magnificent at making speeches
Which tell us of our national glory
The stirring and redeeming story
That we are good and the others bad
That we are happy – the others sad.

Then having said these wondrous things
Our leaders stand like queens and kings
So noble, truthful, just and wise
That tears of gladness fill our eyes.
Until, upon election day
We vote and have them flushed away.

The Departed

Don't fret too much for the departed
Even though they leave you broken-hearted.
Have no fear,
They *will* reappear.

When you're alone and unprepared
They will just turn up. Do not be scared.
Be still. Do not turn away;
There is something wise they have come
   to say.

To you and to you alone;
Some plain and simple thing already known.
They will touch you and say,
'It's all right, everything will be okay.'

Or something just like that, short and clear,
Then casually they will turn and softly
   disappear,
Leaving you elated and in perfect peace;
The meaning of life and death will then
   increase.

And your love for the departed one will grow.
There is so much more you will get to know
About love that is unassailable
So long as you make yourself available.

The Child

The human child at a tender age
Is often placed into a cage
Where it is trained to join the cult
Of acting like a nice adult.

The nice adult then goes all sad
And starts to act a little mad
Until it turns completely wild
And liberates its inner child.

Childhood must be had when young,
Something like when spring has sprung;
Let the birds and angels sing,
Childhood is the time of spring.

Eccentrics

The eccentric is a mysterious creature
Peculiar behaviour is its notable feature
Lost and alone in a world of conformity
Where oddness is seen as a dreadful deformity
Yet, of all the creatures, the true
  nonconformist
Is often the brightest, the boldest and
  warmest.

The Grand Parade

And so we come to the grand parade
Where all the sounds of joy are made
As we finally open every cage
And let the humans out to rage
And dance along with hands on hips
To roll their heads and pout their lips
Characters bright and characters shady
The Prime Minister shall dance with the
    naked lady
The sad old man will be reconciled
With the beautiful truth of his inner child
And sweet Palestinians with sweet Israelis
Will blow fanfares of peace on their ukuleles
Then the human creatures shall finally see
That where there is love — *they are free*.

It is Finished

It is finished.
So let us share
These dear remaining moments;
A tiny scoop of air,
Two more little touches of your hand —
The final touches,
And we'll be there.

It is done
Yet love is here —
Not as it was before,
Beneath a world of fear;
For now the world is just a tiny flower;
The light is true
And love is near.

It is gone:
The living pain,

The steady ache for power,
The agony for gain;
Like a fever which has faded now,
And only light
And love remain.

For love was made
In spite of all,
Piece by lonely piece,
Fragments frail and small,
Dearly held when life was cold and dark;
Now love's the light
That holds it all.

It is there —
It is true;
The final touches now
Will see it gently through;
Two more little touches of your hand —
Love for me
And love for you.